I0441487

WHY YOU SHOULDN'T CALL A POLICE OFFICER "CUTE"

by

Earl Weir

DORRANCE PUBLISHING CO., INC.
PITTSBURGH, PENNSYLVANIA 15222

Dorrance Publishing Co., Inc.
701 Smithfield Street
Pittsburgh, PA 15222
Visit our website at *www.dorrancebookstore.com*

ISBN: 978-1-4349-1785-0
eISBN: 978-1-4349-1704-1

Why You Shouldn't Call a Police Officer "Cute"

An Exposé

by

Earl Weir

THE MAY 20, 2006, INCIDENT

AT THE

HOWARD COUNTY YMCA

On Saturday, May 20, 2006, at about 2:00 PM, I was swimming freestyle at the Howard County YMCA. I was swimming on the north side of lane number 3. I was sharing a lane with a person who could pass me. I was swimming in such a manner that made passing me difficult.

At this time, there was only one pool at this facility.

The pool was setup with the northern two lanes designated as the rented, private "PARTY AREA." There was no lane rope between these lanes. The middle two lanes were designated for "LAP SWIM." These two lanes were separated from each other and the rest of the pool by lane ropes. The southern two lanes were designated as the "RECREATIONAL AREA."

On the 45th length of the 100-length, 2500-yard swim, at the shallow end, while making a turn, I bumped into a flotation device, (such as the lifeguards carry). I stopped to see what was wrong.

Megan, the Aquatics Director, said, "You will have to leave the pool because of 'conduct unbecoming a YMCA member.'" She also yelled, "You will apologize!"

I asked, "Apologize for what?"

She must have informed me that she believed that I had hit a kid. In any case, I remember yelling back at her and saying that there was no way that I had hit a kid because I was swimming in the lap lane and the kids were in the adjacent two lanes reserved for the party.

I left the pool area for the locker room. I showered and got dressed to go downstairs to lift weights. This may have taken fifteen minutes. When I was in the locker room, a YMCA employee came in and asked me to go to the reception desk when I got a chance. His tone and manner were not urgent, but I decided to go to the reception area by the front entrance immediately.

I went to the reception desk and asked what they wanted. The receptionist said that this police officer wanted to talk to me. I found out that her name was J. S. Cree.

Officer Cree said, "I heard that you accidentally brushed up against somebody in the pool."

I told her that I didn't know what she was talking about.

She said, "We have several eyewitnesses."

I said that I didn't remember hitting anybody or anything.

She said, "You do not appear to be under the influence of drugs or alcohol. Why can't you remember the incident?"

I hypothesized zoning out. Zoning out is a widely recognized condition that occurs during formal or informal competition by trained or untrained competitors where all that the competitor sees is the other competitor and the field of competition. Wikipedia defines it as an intense form of mental concentration or visualization that focuses consciousness on a narrow subject.

Sometime early in this interchange, she asked me, "How can you be so calm?" I don't think that I answered this question, but I didn't see how becoming excited would help anything.

She also said, "You don't think that you have done anything wrong." Well, she got that one right.

She asked me several times if there was anybody at the YMCA that was out to get me. I told her that I didn't think so. After consultation with my wife, I have changed my mind on this point.

Officer Cree also said, "You are not taking the situation seriously." Well, she got that one right.

During this interchange, she probably said to me, "Since you can't remember the incident, you may have done it."

I may have answered, "Since I can't remember, I certainly may have."

She went into the employee only area near the reception area and talked to several YMCA employees, including Megan and Jen, the Aquatics Coordinator. This conversation lasted ten to fifteen minutes. When they came out, they seemed quite excited. Megan informed me that I would be allowed to get my clothes and then Officer Cree and her partner would escort me off the property. They informed me that, if I returned, I would be charged with "criminal trespass."

Megan also yelled at me several times, "We will continue to investigate! We will continue to investigate!" I got the impression that this investigation would end on the same day as my funeral. Quite frankly, I thought that would be the end of this incident.

As we walked from the locker room, Officer Cree sarcastically mocked me as a "big competitive swimmer" because of my zoning out hypothesis. I have included below an illustration showing that her words, if not her tone, were correct.

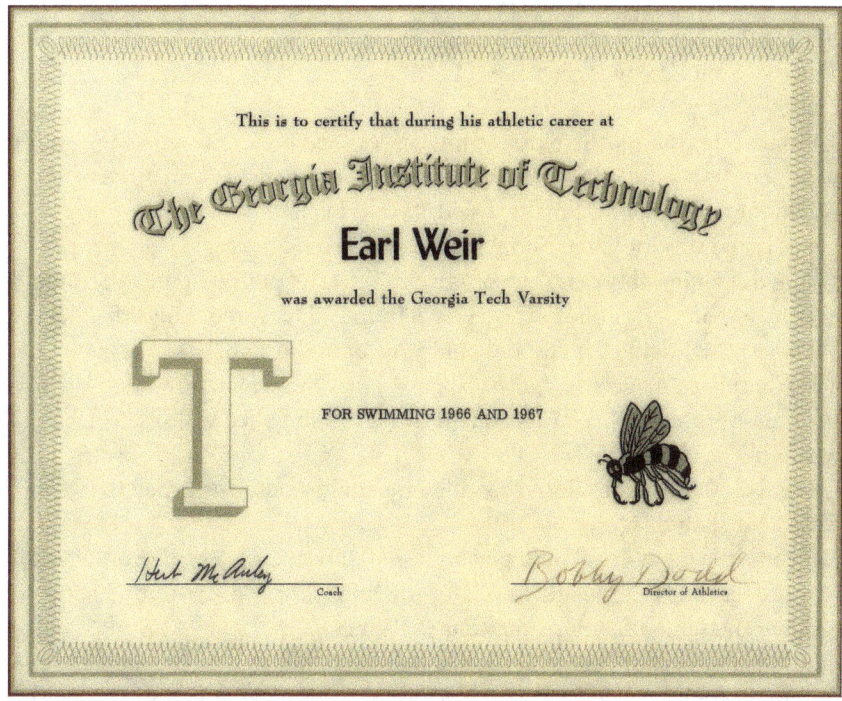

As we walked to my car, Officer Cree continued to harass me by saying, "If you were a man, you would admit what you had done and accept your punishment," and "You are not showing any remorse."

She also said that I should take a course in anger management. This is the same woman, who, about forty-five minutes earlier, had asked me how I could be so calm.

She also advised me to "Find another place to work out." She suggested Bally's or The Columbia Association because they have pools.

Finally, at my car, I asked Officer Cree just exactly what I was accused of doing. She said, "Haven't you been listening?"

Yes, I had been listening. "Accidentally brushed up against somebody" certainly didn't warrant the treatment I was getting.

Then, she told me that I was accused of stopping, standing up, and hitting a five-year-old kid[1] who was in the lap lane. I was amazed, but I had already realized that talking to her made about as much sense as talking to a wall. I got into my car and left.

---

[1] In my opinion, at this point, Officer Cree should have already interviewed the thirteen-year-old Devon and should have been able to make a better estimate of his age.

The Big Mistake

While I was trying to explain to Officer Cree about zoning out, I said that I see only my competitor and the field of competition. I would not see anything else. Then, naïvely, I said to her, "Of course, I would see you."

She asked me, "Why is that, sir?"

I said, "Because you are cute!"

A month later, on our first visit to my lawyer (my wife came with me), after examining the paperwork, he asked me, "What did you do to make this cop so mad at you?"

I thought and thought. Finally, I said, "Well, I called her 'cute.'"

He gave me this look that said, "How could you be so stupid?"

While discussing this case, one of my close friends pointed out, "She should have a thicker skin than that. Police officers have been called worse things than 'cute.'"

Well, yes, "vindictive" is certainly more accurate for her.

The libertarian magazine *Reason*, explained that there is an unwritten law that they call, "contempt of cop." If you transgress this law, the police will find some reason to throw you in the clink.

Of course, Cree had to find a compliant enabling state's attorney to Nifong[2] me. She found Meghan Skaggs.

Officer Cree may be the only person in the universe who has never heard of zoning out. Indeed, the lieutenant, who later investigated my allegations against Officer Cree, called the same phenomenon, tunnel vision.

The fact that, according to Officer Cree, I was calm probably didn't help either. Later, in open court and under oath, Officer Cree claimed that I appeared guilty. What is it about a calm person who isn't showing any remorse, doesn't think that he has done anything wrong, and is not taking the investigation seriously that makes him appear guilty?

The Phone Call

Using my cell phone, I called my wife, Masako, as soon as I could. I told her about the incident and that I was accused of running into a kid.

She said, "Yes. When that happens to me, I will go to the lifeguard and tell him that he isn't doing his job. Then, I will find Jen and tell her that she isn't doing her job and, then, I will find Megan and tell her that she isn't doing her job."

I said, "Yes, I am beginning to understand the problem."

---

[2] A new word derived from the name, Michael Byron Nifong. According to Wikipedia, Mister Nifong is a former North Carolina attorney. He was disbarred due to his misconduct in the 2006 Duke University Lacrosse Case.

I told her that I couldn't remember hitting the kid.
She asked me, "Do you remember an ambulance?"
Ah, I am not a gentle swimmer.

Megan Lehane's Opinion

According to Louis P. Ruzzi, Senior Assistant County Solicitor, Howard County, "Ms. Lehane stated that PFC Cree was stern with Dr. Weir because he was not taking the investigation seriously."

THE ARREST

On Thursday, June 22, 2006, at about 7:30 in the morning, I answered the doorbell. A person with a vest that said, "Police," asked if he and his party could come in. This joint taskforce from the Baltimore and Howard County Police then arrested me on charges of felony assault, among other things.

As soon as I realized what they wanted and where they were taking me, I said to my wife, "Call Sarah and get the name of a good criminal attorney. Then, have him go to the Wilkens Avenue Police Station to get me." The detectives said that would not be necessary since I would probably be released on my own recognizance by the afternoon. I repeated my request to her.

On the way to the police station, the detectives looked over the paperwork. They told me that they were surprised that I had been charged with felony assault and that they had had to serve a warrant. They said, "Howard County is crazy." They thought that I should have been just served a summons to appear in court for, at most, misdemeanor assault.

The detectives also said that, if it was this serious, I should have been arrested on the spot. That is, Officer Cree should not have let me walk away.

At the police station, when the officer was using his radio to try to get somebody to come to the door, instead of using the usual phonetics, he said, "T," as in trumped-up charges.

When I was being booked, one of the detectives said, "There is something here that does not meet the eye. This thing smells rotten to me."

THE COMPLAINT

I found a few things interesting in the paperwork which, by the way, in spite of an intense effort by my lawyer, we did not receive until about August 19. According to my lawyer, the prosecution (hereinafter referred to as the persecution) was extremely reluctant to supply him with the relevant information. He even wrote them a letter asking them for the proper procedure to get this information. I am sure that he was being sarcastic.

My main accuser was a man named Frank Krach. I believe that he called the police using his cell phone. He is the only witness who provided a written statement. I have included it on the next page.

This statement says that the child was approximately six to ten years old. In reality, the young man[3], Devon, according to the police report, was thirteen years old. In my opinion, he was not small for his age.

Mr. Krach wrote, "The lap swimmer did not yield to the child." Well, I have news for Mr. Krach. The lap swimmer was swimming laps in the lap lane. The lap swimmer had the right-of-way. The lap swimmer had reasons to expect that the lifeguard would keep the children in the party area out of the lap lane. Indeed, my computerized dictionary defines a lifeguard as, "An attendant employed at a beach or pool to protect swimmers from *accidents*. [Emphasis Added.]"

I discovered that the YMCA had a surveillance video of the entire incident. I will discuss this subsequently. However, let me summarize here. I will be calling this surveillance video, the "Exonerating Surveillance Video" or ESV. This video shows that the young man neither swam into nor out of the lap lane. Indeed, the lane ropes prevented this. In addition, the persecution claimed that Mr. Taylor could not swim very well.

This was not the first person that I had ever collided with while swimming laps.

---

[3] Judge Mary Reese's opinion—her comments at the end of my trial are in the appendix to this exposé.

However, these collisions were becoming less frequent. I had thought that the lifeguards were, actually, beginning to do their jobs. Unfortunately, the ESV shows that the lifeguards still have no control over the children. As I got older, I slowed down. It is easier to get out of my way.

The other eyewitness was the lifeguard herself. The ESV shows that she was not looking in the direction of the collision when the collision occurred.

Mr. Krach's Written Statement

6

HOWARD COUNTY POLICE DEPARTMENT
VOLUNTARY STATEMENT

1. I.R. # 06-47395	2. Investigating Officer PFC J.S. CREE	3. Nature of the Investigation ASSAULT
4. Statement of: (Last, First, Middle) Krach, Frank, Louis JR		5. Home Address & Telephone # 605 North Bend Dr
6. DOB _,_/5?	7. Sex M	8. Location Where Statement Was Taken Howard County YMCA
9. Date/Time Started 2:55	10. Date/Time Ended 3:05	11. Signature of Officer Taking Statement

12. I, _Frank Krach_, volunteer the following information of my own free will for whatever purpose it may serve.

I watch a sun small (6 to 10 yd) child swim into the lap lane of the pool. The lap swimmer did not yield to the child. The child tried to swim under the lap swimmer who then struck the child with a closed fist from above as the child tryed to swim away. It apeared easily intentional and deliberate. I identified this individual to the officer.

14. Signature of Person Making Statement Frank Krach 5-20-06	15. Signature of Witness

HCPD 2111

8

THE HOWARD COUNTY POLICE REPORT

I have scanned in and included below pages four and five of the Howard County Police Department Narrative Report as prepared by Officer Cree. As you can see on page four, she claimed that Mr. Krach said, "As the child was trying to swim away, the lap swimmer stood up and struck the child with a closed fist, while the child was still under the water."

The phrase, "stood up," is not included in Mr. Krach's written statement and he denied making such a statement while under oath in open court. You should also note that, in the last sentence on page four, Officer Cree unequivocally demonstrates that she was not listening to me.

Interestingly, Officer Cree makes no mention of her partner, PFC A. F. Giardina, until page five of this narrative. It is just as if the other officer did not want to be involved in this incident.

I strongly believe that Officer Cree perjured herself to enhance the incident so that she could charge me with severe charges. She did this to punish me by subjecting me to the public embarrassment and hassle of an arrest rather than a summons. In doing this, Officer Cree abridged my right to due process.

Page Four of the HCP Report

HOWARD C 'NTY POLICE DEPARTMENT NARRAT' REPORT

4

1. P \GE 4 OF 5	TOTAL	2. ☒ CONTINUATION ☐ SUPPLEMENT	2A. TYPE OF INCIDENT ASSAULT	3. CASE NUMBER 06-47395

4. VICTIM/REPORTING PERSON'S NAME (LAST, MIDDLE, FIRST) Taylor, Devon Edward	5. DATE OF REPORT 5/20/2006	TIME OF REPORT 1507	6. RELATED CASE NUMBERS

7. NARRATIVE:

On May 20, 2006 at approximately 1503 hours, PFC J.S. Cree responded to the YMCA located at 4331 Montgomery Road for an assault.

Upon arrival, PFC J.S. Cree made contact with Ms. Megan Lehane, the manager at YMCA. She advised a subject, later identified as Edward Earl Weir W/M DOB 3/9/1945, had assaulted a 13 year old boy in the swimming pool.

PFC J.S. Cree made contact with a witness, Mr. Frank Louis Krach Jr. W/M DOB 1959. He advised the following:
 - He observed a young boy swimming in the lap lane.
 - The boy tried to swim under a lap swimmer.
 - As the child was trying to swim away, the lap swimmer stood up and struck the child with a closed fist, while the child was still under the water.
 - Mr. Krach stated to the officer, that the act appeared intentional.
 - Mr. Krach wrote a written statement, which is attached to this report.

Ms. Lehane stated that a lifeguard, Aleaya Gordon, also observed the entire incident and confirmed Mr. Krach's account of the incident.

PFC J.S. Cree also spoke with Ms. Donna Marie Treash, who also observed the incident. Ms. Treash stated she saw the man hit the boy while the boy was under the water.

Mr. Krach and Ms. Lehane identified the subject to the officer.

PFC J.S. Cree made contact with Mr. Weir, who advised the following:
 - He did not remember ever hitting the boy.
 - He stated he had not had a problem with anyone in the pool.
 - He first became aware of a situation when the lifeguard asked him to leave the pool area.

PFC J.S. Cree asked Mr. Weir if he had any memory problems and he stated no. PFC J.S. Cree asked Mr. Weir if he had any medical conditions that would effect his memory, he stated no. PFC J.S. Cree asked if he was under the influence of any medications that would effect his memory, he stated no. PFC J.S. Cree asked Mr. Weir if he was currently under the influence of any drugs, alcohol, or medications, he stated no.

PFC J.S. Cree asked Mr. Weir if he could provide any explanation as to what had transpired, he stated that he sometimes "zones out". When asked what he refers to, he stated that he becomes unaware of what is going on around him while he swims. During the course of the conversation, Mr. Weir had mentioned swimming with another swimmer, who was faster than he. When asked why he could remember this swimmer when he said that he "zones out", Mr. Weir could not provide an explanation.

8. OFFICER PFC J.S. Cree	9. OFFICER ID 5071	10. DATE 5/21/2006	11. SUPERVISOR Cpl. A.	12. SUPERVISOR ID 4612	13. DATE 5/4/06

14. CASE STATUS ☐ ACTIVE – FOLLOW-UP DUE: _____ ☐ CLOSED/LEADS EXHAUSTED ☒ CLOSED/CLEARED	15. DISPOSITION (ONLY COMPLETE WHEN CASE STATUS = CLOSED/CLEARED) C—

16. FORWARD COPY TO: ☐ CIB ☐ PUBLIC AFFAIRS ☐ V&N ☐ STATE'S ATTY ☐ BUREAU CMDR( ) ☐ YOUTH SECTION ☐ DSS ☐ JSA ☐ CO RISK MGMT ☐ TELETYPE ☐ OTHER( )	17. RECORDS USE

Page Five of the HCP Report

HOWARD COUNTY POLICE DEPARTMENT NARRATIVE REPORT

1 PAGE 5 OF 5	TOTAL	2. ☒ CONTINUATION ☐ SUPPLEMENT	2A.TYPE OF INCIDENT ASSAULT	3 CASE NUMBER 06-47395

4.VICTIM/REPORTING PERSON'S NAME (LAST, MIDDLE, FIRST) Taylor, Devon Edward	5.DATE OF REPORT 5/20/2006	TIME OF REPORT 1507	6 RELATED CASENUMBERS

7. NARRATIVE:

Mr. Weir also stated at one point that if "all these people" are saying I did this, then maybe I did.

PFC J.S. Cree and PFC A.E. Giardina spoke with Devon Edward Taylor. He advised the following:
- He was swimming in the lap lane in the YMCA located in Ellicott City.
- He advised at one point that while under water someone grabbed the back of his shirt from the rear.
- He then was struck in his rear upper left shoulder.
- Devon stated that he was not injured nor did he want any medical treatment.
- He stated that he is an "ok" swimmer, but when asked if he could tread water, he stated that he could not.

According to all witnesses to the incident, the assault took place in the shallow end of the pool. The incident disrupted a birthday party, which Devon was attending, and everyone else in the pool area, including the witnesses PFC J.S. Cree spoke with.

PFC J.S. Cree made contact with Devon's mother, Veronica Sutton, via phone. PFC J.S. Cree advised Ms. Sutton of what transpired and that Mr. Weir was being charged.

Based on the following facts:
- the age of the victim, Devon Taylor 13 year old boy,
- the age of the suspect, Edward Earl Weir, 61 year old male,
- the difference in size between the two, Devon is approximately 60 pounds, Mr. Weirs is approximately 216 pounds,
- the location which the assault took place, the swimming pool of the Ellicott City YMCA,
- the swimming ability of the victim, Devon Taylor,
- and the nature of the assault, striking Devon with a closed fist on his upper rear left shoulder, which is in close proximity to his head.

PFC J.S. Cree will be requesting a warrant for Mr. Weir from the District Court Commissioner. PFC J.S. Cree will be requesting Mr. Weir be charged with the following:
- CR 3-202 - Assault First Degree
- CR 3-203 - Assault Second Degree
- CR 3-204(a)(1) - Reckless Endangerment
- CR 10-201(c)(2) - Disorderly Conduct

RCS: CLOSED

8. OFFICER PFC J.S. Cree	9. OFFICER ID 5071	10. DATE 5/20/2006	11. SUPERVISOR	12. SUPERVISOR ID	13. DATE

14. CASE STATUS ☐ ACTIVE – FOLLOW-UP DUE: _____ ☐ CLOSED/LEADS EXHAUSTED ☐ CLOSED/CLEARED	15. DISPOSITION (ONLY COMPLETE WHEN CASE STATUS = CLOSED/CLEARED)

16. FORWARD COPY TO: ☐ CIB ☐ PUBLIC AFFAIRS ☐ V&N ☐ STATE'S ATTY ☐ BUREAU CMDR( ) ☐ YOUTH SECTION ☐ DSS ☐ JSA ☐ CO RISK MGMT ☐ TELETYPE ☐ OTHER( )	17 RECORDS USE

THE EXONERATING SURVEILLANCE VIDEO (ESV)

Sometime around the first week of June, I learned that the YMCA had a surveillance video of the incident. Somebody reported to me that Troy, the head of the Howard County YMCA, had said that this video was "very incriminating." In spite of this opinion, I immediately wanted to see this video to see what happened. In addition, I was curious as to why the YMCA's investigation was taking so long given that they had a video of the incident.

On Wednesday, June 7, 2006, I sent the following email message to Troy:

> **Subject: Investigation**
>
> **Troy,**
>
> **I have just learned that the pool has a video camera. Given this fact, why is your investigation taking so long?**
>
> **-Earl**

He replied:

> **Subject: RE: Investigation**
> **Date: Wed, 7 Jun 2006 15:43:36 -0400**
> **From: Weaver, Troy**
>
> **I am waiting for the police, to get back to me...**
> **....**
> **Troy S. Weaver**
> **Executive Director**

Howard County Family YMCA
4331 Montgomery Road
Ellicott City, MD 21043
410-465-4334

Briefly, the video shows a young man playing, _**not** swimming_, in the lap lane, which, of course, is against the YMCA rules. As I approached, the young man submerged to avoid a collision. Since I did not see the young man submerge, I swam over him. The young man did not try to swim away but surfaced between the wall and me. Somehow, I sensed the young man and swam around him to get to the wall. I then did the same turn that the video caught me doing both before and after the incident and proceeded on my way. The young man got out, and, after a brief conference with an adult, rejoined the party.

Unfortunately, this type of incident is so common at the Howard County YMCA that we lap swimmers describe lap swimming at the Howard County YMCA as a "contact sport." Most of the time, the lap swimmers do not remember the individual incidences. In any case, I was so concentrating on the swimmer who was sharing my lane that I do not remember either swimming over the young man or swimming around him to get to the wall.

I may appear to standup during an open turn, but the video shows me doing this at every turn. In addition, Officer Cree's narrative has me standing up "while the child is under the water." The video shows me avoiding the young man to make that particular turn and that, as I was making the turn, the young man was clearly standing up.

On page five of the HCP report (shown previously), Officer Cree states that Devon's weight is "approximately 60 pounds." Devon is the same person that Judge Reese, in her summation, before declaring me "not guilty," calls a young man and that the ESV shows standing in three and one-fourth feet of water with the water just above his waist. You may find Judge Reese's comments in the appendix to this exposé.

I have included frames from this video on the next few pages. The video shows that I did not break stride as I swam over the young man. It was just as if I did not see him.

Krach Seemed More Interested in a Girl

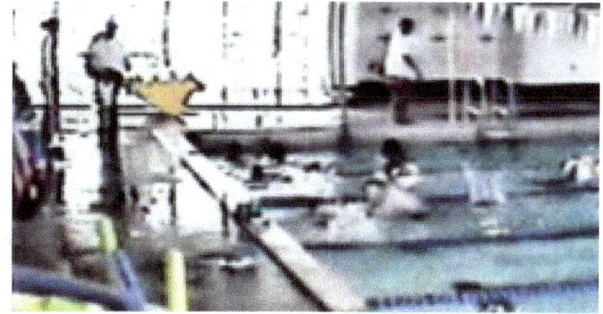

Sixty Pound (?) Young Man Stood in Three and One-Fourth Feet of Water

Well, it is more exciting if you get wet.

The video shows me doing what my lawyer described as an "old style turn." I call it an "open turn." I have since learned, from a swimming coach who is even older than I, that it is a "touch and go" turn.

Please, also note that the young man came up in front of me. If I had touched him with any force, I would have been propelled forward and him rearward, so that he would have come up behind me.

Suppression of the ESV

In the opinion of this cynic, lap swimmers are not as welcomed at the Howard County YMCA as are other individuals. We come frequently but do not take classes, which provide extra income for the YMCA. Yet, we use the facility and require some sense of discipline and cleanliness in the pool and related areas. As discussed above, my wife is particularly insistent that the pool rules be followed.

In my opinion, here is what happened. Officer Cree, the various members of the Howard County YMCA staff, and the so-called eyewitnesses, viewed the video and did not realize its exonerating nature. Megan then supplied Officer Cree with a copy of the video which she took with her. Later, when Officer Cree and the enabling state's attorney viewed the video, they realized the exonerating nature of it and buried it. Of course, they deny this.

The next Monday, Troy, Megan, and perhaps others, also viewed the video and saw the exonerating nature of it. Troy would later tell me, "We just thought that the video was taken from the wrong angle to see the incident." Yea, right, look at those frames. I was born at night, but it wasn't last night. We were in the midst of planning The Counterattack, which is discussed below, so I didn't challenge this ridiculous statement.

In any case, here is what I think should have happened. When Troy et al. viewed the video and realized that nothing happened (it was at the wrong angle), he should have contacted Officer Cree and said something like, "We can't get rid of him and his wife this time because of this video." This is particularly true, since I was soon to know of the existence of the video. Then, Officer Cree should have reconsidered her persecution of me for "contempt of cop."

What did happen is that Troy described the video as "very incriminating" to the wrong person. This person informed me of the video. I immediately demanded to see it because, quite frankly, I wanted to see what happened. The cat was out of the bag.

As described below, I got a lawyer and told him about the video. He immediately wanted to subpoena it. I thought that it was overkill since I still, naïvely, felt that Troy would give me a copy or that the persecution would provide a copy on discovery. I never, in my wildest dreams, thought that Officer Cree would claim that she did not asked for a copy when there were numerous signs that the facility was under constant video surveillance.

As described below, the trial got delayed from September to October because Officer Cree was on vacation. In October, the persecution tried to delay the trial again because Officer Cree wanted to go on vacation again. My lawyer had had enough. He demanded a speedy trial. I have surmised that when the going gets tough, Officer Cree goes on vacation.

The YMCA received the subpoena around the first of August. According to my lawyer, Troy said that they had lost the video, then he said that they had recorded over it. At any rate, the video arrived at my lawyer's office after close of business on October 6, the Friday before my trial on the next Wednesday. I was fortunate that my lawyer was working late that day. It was in an uncommon format that required a codex to run. We got a video expert to get it running on my wife's laptop that Sunday. I cannot run it on my current laptop without expert help.

Wednesday, during the trial, the video would not run on the courtroom video facilities. Fortunately, we had taken our laptop to the courtroom. The judge had to come to the defense table to view the video, which she found exonerating.

Cops and Surveillance Video

In my opinion, police officers should fear video. It gives an unbiased observation; police officers and eyewitnesses often do not. I believe that Earle Stanley Gardner once had one of his characters (perhaps Perry Mason) say, "Circumstantial evidence is the best evidence because you can't fake the circumstances."

Current Surveillance Video at the Y

After renovation, the Y did not reinstall the surveillance video in the pool area. I have heard that this is because, "It causes too much trouble."

THE COUNTERATTACK

Masako and I first visited my lawyer on June 29, 2006. The persecution had not set the date of the trial. I think that they just wanted all this to go away. My lawyer managed to get them to set a date.

During that first visit, my lawyer wondered aloud if Officer Cree had gone "prosecutor shopping." That is, did she have to shop around to find a prosecutor dumb enough to take the case?

I was watching the Military Channel or something like that. It said that officers wear their insignia on their shoulders because they are responsible for the action of the armed forces while NCOs wear their insignia on their sleeves because they are the muscle of the armed forces. Well, once, I wore chrome-plated "railroad tracks" on the epaulets of my green "blouse."

Sometime around the first of September, I was walking my dog in the woods. Suddenly, I felt the full weight of those railroad tracks on my shoulders, and not the chrome-plated kind, the steel and timber kind. As I staggered under this weight, I realized that Cree was a rogue cop. I realized that she would probably try to railroad somebody else who may not have an ESV available. I realized that she had to be stopped. I looked around for somebody to stop her. I was the only one there. Officers hate it when that happens. In addition, I realized that the people who cooperated with her attempt at a miscarriage of justice, particularly the enabling state's attorney, had to be made uncomfortable. I believe that the enabling state's attorney in this case should have been disbarred, particularly for suppressing the ESV.

The Trial

I have always maintained that the persecution had the ESV from day one, and, when its exonerating nature became apparent, buried it. The YMCA had many signs stating that the facility was under video surveillance. Only the most incompetent would not have asked if such a video existed. Interestingly, they have to argue that they are incompetent while I argue that they are vindictive.

The night before the trail, my lawyer telephoned me and told me that the persecution had offered us a deal. He said that it was a very good deal, but he suggested that I not take it.

Just before the trial, the persecution said that, if I would accept a stet, they would recommend ten hours of community service. My lawyer seemed quite proud that he had negotiated this deal for me.

I thought and thought. I weighed the possible twenty-five years of jail time versus ten hours of community service.

During this process, my lawyer said, "I like to fight, but at the end of the day, I get to go home even if I lose."

A couple of years later, when I was in Saint Petersburg, caring for my mother, I had occasion to discuss this statement with Masako. I emailed her, "He doesn't like to fight. He likes to negotiate. I like to fight."

She emailed me, "Doesn't to fight mean to negotiate and persuade?"

I emailed her, "My dear Masako, to a Captain, US Army, Field Artillery, to fight does **NOT** mean to negotiate and persuade!"[4]

Ah, herein, I am presenting evidence that it is not advisable to try to railroad a guy that already has railroad tracks. We have evidence that the persecution extensively looked into my background. Experimental evidence indicates that, as soon as they saw those railroad tracks, they should have backed off. Perhaps they were zoned out or had developed tunnel vision and could not conceive quitting.

Let's get back to the story. I had decided that being found not guilty would help The Counterattack. After much soul-searching, I committed to The Counterattack. There would be a trial and I would be found not guilty.

Ah, it seems to me that neither my lawyer nor the persecution was prepared to go to trial. The Counterattack seemed to achieve the element of surprise...perhaps, a little too well.

Internal Affairs

On the next page, I have included a letter that I sent to Internal Affairs at the Howard County Police. The page after that is the Executive Summary of the accompanying documentation. I think that they make interesting reading. The case was assigned to Lt. Gregory R. Scott of the Howard County Police.

Now, I believe that "Ms. Shinham" also had railroad tracks.

---

[4] In case anybody is interested to the guy in the green suit with the railroad tracks on his epaulets and crossed tubes (ah, cannon barrels) on his lapels, to fight means to find, fix, and destroy.

Edward Earl Weir, II, Ph.D.

---

602 Saint Johnsbury Road   (410) 788-8217
Baltimore, MD 21228-4046   mdweir@yahoo.com

January 18, 2007

Ms. Karen Shinham
Howard County Police Department, Internal Affairs Division
3410 Court House Drive
Ellicott City, MD 21043

Dear Ms. Shinham:

I am enclosing a narrative, surveillance video, and other documentation of what, in my opinion, is a vendetta against me by PFC J. S. Cree of the Howard County Police Department. Because I did not treat her with the respect that she expected, she exaggerated and fabricated eyewitness testimony and ignored exculpatory evidence. She then charged me with crimes so atrocious that even her manufactured evidence could not justify, in the opinion of all of the legal experts whom I consulted, the severity of the charges.

On October 11, 2006, without me having to testify, Judge Mary Reese found me "not guilty" of these charges.

I believe that PFC Cree's obvious abuse of her Police Authority is intolerable in a free society.

I will be out of town for my mother's ninetieth birthday from Thursday, January 31, until about Monday, February 12. If you wish to meet with me, Thursdays are the best days. I would like to bring my wife with me to our meeting since she can get the video running. In addition, she understands the situation at the Howard County YMCA and the quirks in my personality, including my macabre jokes, which make some people despise me.

If you need more information, I have at least 68 pages of narratives and correspondence with my attorney, Mr. Tom O'Connell, on this matter.

Thank you for your prompt attention to this matter. I hope to meet with you soon.

Case Number 06-47395

Executive Summary:

This complaint documents PFC J. S. Cree's overzealous persecution of me, Dr. Edward Earl Weir, II. Because I did not treat her with the respect she expected, Officer Cree lied about eyewitness testimony in her charging document, and, in court and under oath, lied about my demeanor during her interrogation. She also charged me with preposterously severe crimes, apparently without investigation, or, worse, after suppressing exculpatory evidence, a video surveillance of the incident. I have attached copies of the charging documents, the video of the incident, and a CD of the proceedings of my trial in which I was found, "not guilty."

Perhaps the best indication of PFC Cree's attitude towards me is Judge Mary Reese's Summation Comments. These comments begin at 18:16:15 on the enclosed CD. She said, "I also think [Mister Taylor's] recollection has been enhanced or supplanted by the number of adults that have been involved in this." I believe that this "number of adults" includes PFC Cree.

Judge Reese also said, "So, I don't doubt Devon's testimony at all, but I do think that the adults in this situation have made it a much, quote, unquote, 'bigger deal' than this incident really was."

Furthermore, she said, "Even with the testimony of Officer Cree, and I will note that that occurred during a thirty to forty-five minute time period, that he was, Mister Weir was, told that he couldn't leave the YMCA until she finished her investigation. Which, quite frankly, he could leave if he wasn't under arrest; he should have felt free to leave, although, from her testimony, I could tell that she wasn't going to let him."

In addition, Judge Reese said, "Devon's own reality of what had happened was lost because of all the...I am going to use the word 'fuss' that all these adults put on him."

-- End of Executive Summary --

Around the first of March, Masako and I met with Lt. Scott and gave him a package of information about the incident. We also gave him a copy of the ESV and a copy of the CD of the court proceedings. He promised to look into the matter.

On April 25, 2007, Lt. Scott called and left a message on our answering device. In part, he said:

> I have completed all of the interviews that I need to do except for the interview with the officer. She's been on vacation for the last two weeks. [Again?] So, I am working hard to get an interview date scheduled for her. Because it is a possible disciplinary issue, she is entitled to an attorney under Maryland Law, the Law Enforcement Officer's Bill of Rights. So, I am working to get an ap-

pointment with her and her attorney to interview her and then it will be finished. I just got to finish typing it up. So, I am hoping that I can get her in for an interview the end of this week or next week at the very, very latest. So, that is the only thing that is holding it up. I got to interview Officer Cree and she is entitled to an attorney and she wants an attorney present. I am just trying to get that scheduled as soon as possible.

Having to have an attorney to talk to your superior must be a real great career move.

Internal Affairs Response:

I have scanned in and included on the next page Howard County's response. This letter arrived at our house sometime in August in an envelope postmarked July 31, 2007. However, the letter is dated January 24, 2007. Here is a possible scenario:

McMahon to lackey: "Please prepare a letter which addresses the concerns of this concerned citizen."

After downloading and printing the usual, stonewalling, boilerplate malarkey, lackey: "Here you go, boss!"

McMahon: "Oh, wait a minute! We have to investigate before we send it!"

Also, please note that the letter is not signed. It has "for Major Bender" over McMahon's printed signature.

In my opinion, malarkey like this gives all police supervisors a bad name.

envelope postal stamp
7/31/07

KEN ULMAN
County Executive

WILLIAM J. MCMAHON
Chief of Police

HOWARD COUNTY DEPARTMENT OF POLICE
3410 Courthouse Drive, Ellicott City, MD 21043

January 24, 2007

Edward Earl Weir II, Ph.D.
602 Saint Johnsbury Road
Baltimore, Maryland 21228-4046

Dear Dr. Weir:

I am responding to your complaint concerning allegations of improper performance against Police Officer First Class Jennifer Cree from an incident that took place at the YMCA located in Ellicott City, Maryland on May 20, 2006. I apologize for the extended length of the investigation that included several contacts outside of the police department; however, I wanted to ensure a fair and thorough conclusion.

The case initiated by PFC Cree was taken before a court commissioner and reviewed by the State's Attorney's Office who ultimately was the deciding entity to proceed with the case to trial. A judge presided over the case and made a ruling exonerating you from the charges. Your allegation was investigated by a supervisor in the Operations Command and based upon the findings and conclusion of that investigation I have determined the facts are insufficient to support the charge of improper performance or perjury by PFC Cree. The internal investigation did highlight a need for enhanced training for our officers in differentiating the requirements for charging the different degrees of assault. As you can expect, there are numerous scenarios that officers deal with on a daily basis in which they are expected to apply the law. Thus, I have directed our training staff to develop an improved guideline for the officers.

I want to thank you for bringing your situation to my attention. If you have any questions concerning this matter, please contact Lieutenant B. E. Donovan, Commander – Internal Affairs Division, at 410-313-5800.

Sincerely,

for Major Bender

William J. McMahon
Chief of Police

WJM:BED:bw

(410) 313-2203
(410) 313-2272
WWW.HCPD.ORG
HCPD@CO.HO.MD.US

Nationally Accredited Since 1990

Suing for False Arrest

We then tried to sue Howard County for false arrest. We could not get a lawyer to take us seriously. However, we did get the lawyers for Howard County to see the ESV. Howard County is just able to throw up too many roadblocks to justice.

Specifically, we sent the following email to the only one of them that we could get to take our money:

> Dear Dr. Christian *[Doctor of Jurisprudence]*,
> Masako has tried to call you a few times. Your automated receptionist seems to be out of whack.
> We would like YOU to review the Exonerating Surveillance Video (ESV) of the non-incident that occurred at the Howard County YMCA on May 20, 2006. Perhaps, then, you may understand why we are enraged about Ms. Cree's abuse of her Police Powers. Then, you may acknowledge the importance of our action against her, the Enabling state's attorney, the Howard County Police Department, and the Howard County YMCA. We believe that this case has striking similarities to the Duke Lacrosse case. We may not get a similar response; nonetheless, we believe that we should try. The police and state's attorney who are supposed to protect society abused their trusted power for their own agenda. This is intolerable in our society. We are extremely annoyed with the Police Chief's response to our complaint. It is simply a form letter and completely ignores our point.

Suing the Government

I have since learned from a lawyer—to whom I gave a manuscript of this exposé—that government limits the amount of damages that you can get from them. Government also limits the lawyer's fees.

Death of J. S. Cree

On or about Sunday, November 22, 2009, J. S. Cree's brother found her body in her home in Columbia, Maryland. Her funeral was at the Gary L. Hoffman Funeral Home. As with John Wilkes Booth, her cause of death and burial place are closely guarded secrets. Neither experts in Internet searching techniques for this information nor I could locate her death certificate.

The information that I have indicates that the official position on the cause of death may have been an undiagnosed "medical condition." Well, one of her grandfathers had a medical condition that allowed him to live to the ripe old age of 103. (That is, one hundred and three years, not minutes.) Ms. Cree was thirty-one when she died.

I believe that Officer Cree died by her own hand. Indeed, exsanguination caused by excessive wrist slashing could be considered a medical condition. We already know that Officer Cree was a very controlling person and suicide is controlling the uncontrollable.

If she died by her own hand, how much did The Counterattack influence her decision? Well, when I met her in May 2006, she had one stripe on her sleeve and she was a PFC when she died. That is, she was not promoted after May 2006. According to the November 24, 2009, *Baltimore Sun,* "Cree was recognized for outstanding work in memorandums of recognition in July 2002 and April 2003. She was nominated for Police Officer of the Month in December 2003." I could find no other commendations for her after 2003. I believe that she was a PFC in 2003. Her photo on her Internet Obituary shows her wearing a cap that may represent the New York City Police Department.

She was a cowgirl. Cowgirls do not do anything by halves. They always do something outstanding, either good or bad. On December 17, 2006, using lights and siren, she barreled through a red light and hit an SUV hard enough to flip it onto a third vehicle.

Prevention of the Premature Death of J. S. Cree

Howard County Police Response:
One of the Primary Objectives of The Counterattack was to get what I believed to be a rogue cop off the Howard County Police Force. Indeed, this objective was realized, although not as I had hoped. Firing her would have been more effective in discouraging this behavior in other potentially rogue cops. Tossing her in jail for perjury would have been even more effective.

Kids in the Lap Lane:
The YMCA could have enforced its own rules against kids in the lap lane.

Adult Reaction:
The "brief conference with an adult," mentioned previously, in my opinion, should have gone something like this:
Kid: "That mean man hit me!"
Adult: "Well, stay out of the lap lane. What do you want me to do about it?"
Unfortunately, in Howard County, kids are allowed to do anything that they please.

Krach's Nonsense:
Some responsible adult, preferably Cree, might have picked up on Mr. Krach's "the lap swimmer did not yield," and description of the normal sized thirteen-year-old Devon as, "small (6 to 10 y[ears] o[ld])"—nonsense. I wonder how Devon feels at being called, "small."

The Exonerating Surveillance Video:

In a meeting in January 2007, Troy said that he had called Cree several times and left messages about the video and that his calls were unanswered. Indeed, Masako called Cree several times and left messages detailing how and why the management of the YMCA was out to get me, and these calls similarly went unanswered. So, she just may not have answered her voice mail.

There is absolutely no doubt in my mind that, if Troy had described the video as "very incriminating," as he did to at least one of my close friends, Cree would have used lights and siren and probably run over a kid on a bicycle to come and get it. However, he must have described it differently in his voice mail to Cree.

Once the persecution realized that I knew about the ESV, they should have backed off. If this had happened, I would not have had to make Officer Cree play the fool to her superiors and to endanger the careers of other members of the persecution or, as I like to call them, The Coven.

McMahon's Response:

If, instead of using standard operating procedure by trying to sweep it under the rug, McMahon realized that this incident was a cry for help from Officer Cree. Surely, the Howard County Police Department has a psychiatrist or psychologist (aka shrink) that might have been able to help Cree.

APPENDIX

Kids in the Lap Lanes at the Howard County YMCA

The incident occurred because children, who are not lap swimmers, are allowed unrestricted access to the lap lanes at the Howard County YMCA. The subpoenaed video clearly shows this problem.

These incidences are so common that I have become desensitized to the point of making macabre jokes, and Masako has invoked the wrath of the managers, Megan and Jen, the lifeguards, and, eventually and indirectly, Officer Cree by constantly complaining that these people should, "do their job and keep the kids out of the lap lane."

I have observed that, if a lifeguard does the job and makes the offending kid leave and, then, the parent complains, the lifeguard's decision is overturned and the lifeguard is disciplined.

Masako and I believe that endangering children by not restricting their access to an area where they may be injured is criminal.

My Insensitivity to Kids in the Lap Lane

After reading a manuscript of this exposé, one of my close friends commented that one reason that Officer Cree and the rest of The Coven were annoyed with me is because I did not seem to care about the kid's welfare. Indeed, as described by Officer Cree, being calm, not showing any remorse, not thinking that he has done anything wrong, and not taking the investigation seriously is not the attitude appropriate for a person who has just been informed by a police officer that he is suspected of running into a small[5] child. I did not even bother to ask if the kid was okay.

---

[5] Mister Krach's description, not mine.

I believe that this callousness stems from my strong belief that the staff of the Howard County YMCA cannot keep the pool safe for the undisciplined children. I recall a couple of incidences that occurred before I developed this attitude.

Lifeguard Admits that She Cannot Control the Children

Long, long ago, when I was younger, there was a lifeguard who I will accurately describe as tempting jailbait. I only took advantage of her attitude once. I wanted to swim, but there was no lifeguard scheduled. She volunteered to stay after her shift and to watch me swim.

Another time, she was on duty. My friend was swimming his laps. I was watching. A teenage girl, tempting jailbait herself, was, ah, playing in the lap lane, perhaps trying to attract this man's attention. Ah, he was, ah, young and not ugly—just smart. He was not paying that much attention to her.

I went to my friendly lifeguard and asked, "What are you doing? Are you waiting for him to hit her?"

She said, "Yes! There is nothing that I can do about it!"

My Last Attempt to Protect Kids at the Howard County YMCA

Long ago, I was swimming my laps. An idiot sent his kid down the lane behind me. I turned at the wall and almost smacked right into the kid. I got out and colorfully described to the idiot exactly what I thought of his mental capacity. I was kicked out of the pool and the Howard County YMCA for thirty days. I went to swim at a different YMCA.

Let me emphasize this: I was kicked out. The idiot was allowed to stay.

This is the last time that I can remember worrying about large kids in the lap lane at the Howard County YMCA. If the Howard County YMCA does not care, why should I? However, I do remember seeing two girls in the play area on May 20, 2006. Even in my focused condition, I remember thinking that I had better look out for them. I would put their ages at four to six years old or minus three in Krach Years.

I mentioned this incident to Officer Cree. I wondered why it did not come up later in my persecution. Now, I realize why. Not only does the incident demonstrate that I once cared about the welfare of kids at the YMCA, but also it demonstrates that the conditions at the Howard County YMCA Pool have chronically been chaotic.

Please note that I append this information to this exposé. As noted in the main report, my wife's attitude has not devolved to this state.

Troy's Options with the Exonerating Surveillance Video

For the sake of argument, let us say that Troy and his staff briefly reviewed the ESV and found it, "very incriminating." Now, what are his options?

- Option 1: He is obsessed with his members and does not care about the transitory people who occasionally rent the YMCA facilities. In this case, he burns the video. He threatens to do the same to any staff member who mentions the video. If the police figure out that there may be such a video, he says that he has already recorded over it.

- Option 2: He favors his members over the transitory people who occasionally rent the YMCA. In this case, he does not volunteer the video to the police. He immediately informs the member that he has the video and supplies the member with a copy.
- Option 3: He is neutral. In this case, he supplies copies of the video to the police and the member.
- Option 4: He is slightly anti-member. In this case, he supplies the video to the police. When the member's attorney subpoenas the video, he supplies it immediately.
- Option 5: He is extremely anti-member. In this case, he volunteers the video to the police. When the member's attorney subpoenas it, he first objects that he does not have the time to come to the trial. When the member's attorney says that he does not have to come to the trial, he just has to send the video; he says that he has lost it. When that position becomes untenable, he claims that he is looking for it. When that position becomes untenable, he, finally, sends the video to the member's attorney. However, he does this long after the original trial date. The video arrives, as a CD, at the member's attorney's office after the close of business on a Friday, just before the trial on the next Wednesday. The key to deciphering the video is hidden on the CD. Fortunately, for the member, his close friend and the member's wife are quite knowledgeable at making computers work. The member, his attorney, wife, and close friend view the video and cannot find any evidence of a crime. The next Wednesday, Judge Mary Cecilia Reese views the video and determines that the member is "not guilty."

Ah, which option did Mr. Weaver choose? Ah, Option 5.

Judge Mary Reese's Conclusions

At the end of my trial, the judge said the following:

I want to start with Devon's testimony.

I had a thirteen-year-old young man standing before me and, you know, I think that he testified truthfully today. And, I think that he testified to the best of his recollection. But, I also think his recollection has been enhanced or supplanted by the number of adults that have been involved in this. And, I think that's trash.

There is not a doubt in my mind that Mr. Weir probably did touch him when he was swimming his laps. I asked to see the tape again prior to Mr. Weir coming into contact with Devon before the incident occurred. And I asked to see that for a couple of reasons. Number one, I wanted to see what I could tell about Mr. Weir's hands and about his stroke. And, I wanted to see both before the incident and after the incident. And, I will tell you from the tape, from that DVD, that I saw; it looks very consistent to me, both before and after. So, I don't doubt Devon's testimony at all, but I do think that the adults in this situation have made it a much, quote, unquote, 'bigger deal' than this incident really was.

When I look at Mr. Krach, and I think that he thought that he was doing the right thing. I think that he testified truthfully, and, when he was cross examined about what he could see through the water, he said that there was not a lot of splash or moving of the water and I will note that Ms. Gordon says that there was. As a matter of fact, her testimony was that there were a lot of bubbles. But, then he said, when he was further crossed on it, that, regarding his left hand, that it was difficult to tell, it appeared that he made contact, but he appeared to be quite uncertain of that.

But, Devon tells me that there was contact, and, quite frankly, I believe that there was contact, but then the contact, the question for me becomes was this an intentional assault, was it a criminal assault?

Even with the testimony of Officer Cree, and I will note that that occurred during a thirty to forty-five minute time period, that he was, Mr. Weir was, told that he couldn't leave the YMCA until she finished her investigation. Which, quite frankly, he could leave if he wasn't under arrest; he should have felt free to leave, although, from her testimony, I could tell that she wasn't going to let him. He told her that he was not aware of the incident, but then, after thirty to forty-five minutes, he said, 'if all these people are saying that I did this, then, maybe, I did.' Well, that doesn't tell me that there was a big confession. Having represented individuals who are being cross examined by a police officer, I don't find that to be a confession at all. I find that, really, to be a wearing down, and it is just easier to agree with what everybody else is telling you for, after a while, your own, Devon's own reality of what had happened was lost because of all the…I am going to use the word 'fuss' that all these adults put on him. He couldn't remember that he was playing with the ball, which I saw on the screen. He couldn't remember Mr. Weir at all. He couldn't even identify him here today. And, I don't think that he does remember him. I think he remembers the focus on him at the Y. I think that he is certainly going to remember today. So, I don't perceive him to have been lying. I just perceive that the adult perception had been weighed upon him. I am finding Mr. Weir 'not guilty.'

An Alternate Explanation for Officer Cree's Behavior

After reading a manuscript of this exposé, one of my close friends proposed an alternative explanation. Officer Cree's frequent vacations could be explained by a drug addiction. She simply did not want anybody to know that she was visiting a drug rehabilitation center.

In addition, her behavior on December 17, 2006, when "she barreled through a red light and hit an SUV hard enough to flip it onto a third vehicle," could be explained by diminished capacity.

Her death could be a drug overdose. Of course, Howard County would want to suppress this fact.

Masako's Notes (Unedited)

Masako's
Start typing July 1, 2006
Note for the incident Earl was accused of on May 20, 2006 around 3 P.M. at Howard County YMCA

District Court of Maryland for Howard County
Case number   005T00049985
Incident number   06-47395
Reporting Officer   J.S. CREE, female

Saturday, May 20, 2006
Earl called me at the office, informed me that he was kicked out of the Y Megan and Police alleged him hitting a 5 years boy, stood up and hit him with a fist. Earl denied any knowledge of it. I asked him similar question several times. He completely denied any wrong doing at the Y. When he described what he was accused of and how they claimed he did it, I felt the accusation does not make any sense. He stood up and hit a 5 years old boy with his fist?!?! It is impossible! That was my reaction. It happened in a lap lane and Megan, aquatic director, not lifeguard stooped him with floating device. I have been married him for 21 years and known him for 24 years. He might be off with his joke but he is very kind to other people.

I arrived at Y around 6 P.M. or a little before. When I scanned my membership card, computer alarm went off. A receptionist told me that I could not go in to the facility because your husband had an incident this afternoon. I said; I have been working all day and on my way home, stopped by to swim. (Young Caucasian, light hair, medium to tall height medium weight) I had not done anything that prohibit/banned me to use Y facility. After few more conversation, she let me in. There were 4 other strangers were around listening our conversation. On the way out I asked the same girl, what I should do to be able to use the facility. She said; call Troy on Monday.

As I came home, Earl repeated the same. He did not do or remember what Police and Megan blamed to him. If he did what they say, he thought he should have injury or blouse on his hand. There was no mark on his hands. I took picture of his hands. To make sense to myself, I asked him to explain in detail of the incident. He was sharing a lap lane with one other person. He was saying that they will sort out soon nothing worry about. He also mentioned that the police asked him "do you know that any one out to get you at the Y?" I said of course! I got worry more. Unfortunately, at the time no other regular swimmer was around to tell me this incident. I decided to get a police report before I will do anything to understand the allegation.

Sunday, May 21, 2006

I started search on Internet how to get a police case report.

I went to Y to swim. When alarm goes off at that check in I had similar conversation with the receptionist while strangers listening.

It does not make any sense; I have to find out what really happened at the Y.

Monday, May 22, 2006

I went to Y. The same process, alarm and conversation with the receptionist. I asked for Troy. She told me that Troy is in the staff meeting so could not ask to come to talk to me. I asked to read the journal carefully, if it mentions anything about wife banned from the Y. She said that I know what it says because I entered. At the end, she obliged to my request and found that I could go in. On the way out I asked the girl her name, Briar? When I was going out they are working on the computer at the receptionist; a technician, Tory, Megan, Jen, and some others.

Tuesday May 23, 2006

Visit Howard County Police Head Quarter, first thing in the morning—Parking meter 10¢

I handed to a young policeman a REPORT REQUEST. He consulted an older policeman if it looks O.K.—He said, yes. I asked how to request to talk the police Ms. Cree who wrote this case report. He gave me a phone number to leave a message. Also, he offered to take a message to her, I did leave a note to him that requesting her to call me.

No call from officer Cree.

I worried that when I visit other Y in other region what embarrassment I would face at check in. I have been using other Ys when I visit other state.

Wednesday May 31, 2006

Called officer Cree, left message.

No call from officer Cree.

(June 2, 2006) Case report request and $5 check were returned. Check marked on "You were not involved in the incident, therefore, the report cannot be released to you"

(June 3, 2006) Earl requests the case report in mail.

Wednesday June 7, 2006
Called officer Cree, left message.
No call from officer Cree.

Wednesday June 14, 2006
Called Officer Cree's supervisor, corporal Shaffer, left message.

Thursday June 15, 2006
Early in the morning, corporal Shaffer returned my call. He said, he will tell officer Cree to call me back, if I have more trouble, call him back. He also said that Officer Cree has been out latter part of May.
Officer Cree never called.

(June 17, 2006) Earls Case report request was returned. Check marked "Approval from the State's Attorney's office was needed before this report could be released and approval to release was denied. You must comply with the formal discovery rules through the Howard County States Attorney Office"

Monday June 19, 2006
I understood nothing why we could not get the case report. I start calling offices at Howard County record office, attorney's, commissioners, circuit court clerk, etc. No record of criminal case under Edward Weir. I found that because this case involve minor so that they cannot release the report. I still do not understand that if Earl was accused of doing something and due to that he was banned from all YMCA facility could not obtain the police report. Why cannot defend himself? Also I have been humiliated every day I visit Y and agonizing about this incident, why I cannot learn what had happened and what we were accused of, I do not understand.

Wednesday June 21, 2006
I debated to call Officer Cree but thought it will be no use.

Thursday June 22
A LITTLE AFTER 7 A.M. 4 police/detectives knocked the door, wake me up, they came in handcuffed Earl took him to Wilkins precinct. I hold on to Coco, our

dog, who was barking at the police. I said that it does not make any sense. Detective Jeffery L. Price gave me a card with case # and warrant case # with phone number on it. I had medical appointment on that morning. As soon as I came home I checked answering machine. Police station's phone number was busy, busy, and busy. With ABC map I made Wilkins precinct. First time I read Warrant and Statement of Charges…It still does not make any sense. I am very upset with Y aquatic staff because I am vocal critic of their poor job for a long time, and simply blaming their fault to Earl, Officer Cree who does not have capability to make fair judge; influenced by the squeaking girls, and Earl who is ignorant to contemporary social norm to give them such excuse. I thought, that someone thought need to teach a lesson to Earl.

After we scanned the arrest warrant, statement of charges, and application for statement of charges, we realized that we do not have any idea what it means and what to do. Realized that we need a lawyer. Called Sarah's husband, retired lawyer. We agreed that we need to have a lawyer but did not know any specific person. Earl visited neighbor acquaintance, retired police, for recommendation. He suggested attorney Thomas O'Connell.

Friday June 23, 2006

In the morning Earl called O'Connell, left message. I was too upset with the situation; I called EPA at the office. The representative arranged emergency session with Doctor Long, Psychological consultant, and gave me a lawyer referral from CLS.

In the evening, we decided that we wait attorney O'Connell until Monday and call him back, if he has not called before then.

Earl said he needs to buy a new suit. I said we need to have haircut, etc.

Saturday June 24, 2006

Called attorney Andrew Fontanella, left message. (From CLS)

Monday June 26, 2006

Went to Dr. Long's session. He gave me another lawyer's name.

Earl called Attorney O'Connell, left message.

Attorney Fontanella called back me at home while I was at work. Earl called me at work and made appointment with him on Tuesday, June 27 2006 at 10 A.M.

Tuesday June 27, 2006

We drove to attorney's office in downtown Baltimore. Arrived around 9:30 A.M. Parking meter $1

We talked more than one hour about the case. We learned about the legal system a little. We told him that we are shopping around the lawyers and we will make a decision to whom to ask to represent us within this week.

Since attorney O'Connell has not called back Earl visited neighbor and asked if he has been on vacation. Answer was no.

I called several lawyers offices which I found in the Internet. In the afternoon, attorney O'Connell called back. We made appointment on Thursday 29th at 10 A.M.
Wednesday June 28, 2006
    We had haircut.

Thursday June 29, 2006
    We went attorney O'Connell's office talked more than two hours. Asked him to take our case. Earl wrote a check for $1,000. I felt a little relieved, thinking it is out of our hand. We do not have any idea what and when going to happen to this charge. He was wondering why Earl was charged so heavily. Whoes toe did he step on?
    I have been having trouble to keep calm, distressed. I think I should get out of this situation/marriage which I have been considering quite a while. I strongly believe that Earl and I were treated unjustly on this case. I have to get justice, first!! Otherwise I will not be able to have peace in my mind.

Tuesday July 4, 2006
    Bank of America's statement shows June 15th Y charged family membership fee $72 for both of us. Earl has been prohibited to use Y since May 20, 2006. Officer Cree told him that if he steps on Y property he will be criminally charged.
    Why?

Wednesday July 5, 2006
    Went Y. The check in computer did not make alarm statement. I wondered what happening? It has been set up to publicly embarrass me for 44-45 days. What has happened? I am very suspicious.
    Received in a mail a copy of letters Attorney O'Connell sent to State's Attorney's Office, MVA, and District Court of Maryland Howard County, dated June 30, 2006.

Reason's Tidbits
From Volume 43 (4) August/September 2011, page 13:

Shane Rhooms spent three weeks in jail after New York City police offices identified him as the man who shot at them when they spotted him smoking marijuana in Brooklyn. Fortunately for Rhooms, security video and cell phone records showed he was attending a concert in Manhattan at the time of the shooting. Police officials say they stand by the officers and still think Rhooms is guilty.

Illustrations by Terry Colon